Saskatchewan

Saskatchewan

J. E. Jones

Whitecap Books
North Vancouver, B.C.

Canadian Cataloguing in Publication Data

Main entry under title:

Saskatchewan

ISBN 0-920620-44-2 (bound). — ISBN
  0-920620-45-0 (pbk.)

1. Saskatchewan — Description and travel —
1950-   — Views.* I. Jones, J. E. (Jeanette
Elaine), 1945-
FC3512.S37   917.124′0022′2   C83-091097-2
F1071.8.S37

ISBN 0-920620-44-2 Hardcover
ISBN 0-920-620-45-0 Paperback

Designed by Michael E. Burch
Printed by D. W. Friesen & Sons Ltd.
Altona, Manitoba

© **Whitecap Books Ltd.**
1086 W. 3rd Avenue
North Vancouver, B.C., Canada

First Edition 1983

Printed in Canada

Foreword

Saskatchewan is a province whose citizens are justly proud of her natural blessings and great achievements. This "sleeping giant" is made up of an immense diversity of human and natural resources, with a distinguished past and boundless future. Saskatchewan people have a vision of what we can be and the vitality to make that vision reality. They are the cornerstones of that future.

"Saskatchewan" is a book that affords its readers a glimpse of the many faces of our great province and a feeling for the diversity that is, at once, our strength and our challenge.

Grant Devine
Premier

An Introduction to the Province

Saskatchewan is a land that truly takes its character from the elemental stuff of existence: the earth and the sky.

In ancient times bison fattened on the abundant grasses of the fertile plain, providing for the needs of wandering tribes of Indians. Much later, Europeans came, attracted by the vast, rich plains. The land was broken to agricultural use, a storehouse of plenty, providing not just for the needs of the settlers, but for others across the land. Then the riches beneath the earth's surface were discovered: coal, oil and potash. Today Saskatchewan produces 60% of Canada's wheat crop, and is the world's largest supplier of potash, a major ingredient in fertilizer.

Complementary to the land is the sky, a stage on which are enacted all the dramas that wind and weather can command. The weather in all its permutations is of overwhelming importance to this agricultural province; sunshine and moisture are the two essential ingredients to the crops which are the backbone of its economy. History has shown what power the weather has over the land: the spectre of drought is still sered into the memories of those who farmed during the 1930s. This is not a temperate climate, where seasons blur easily into one another, but a climate of extremes: brilliant sunshine, breathtaking cold, enervating heat, and all accompanied by the ever-present winds of the prairies, from the welcome, cooling breezes of summer to winter's bitter winds, to the miracle of the 'chinook', the melting wind which flows from the west, bringing the promise of spring.

Saskatchewan is a land of contrasts. The broad, agricultural belt separates the northern half of the province from a unique and surprising strip at the far south. The north is an almost untouched wilderness, a land of lakes and rivers where Saskatchewan's history began. The passage of the early explorers left no trace upon the land, but it opened up the west for further development. The south contains the Great Sand Hills, a 700 square mile (1,813 square kilometre) area of shifting sand, the Cypress Hills, a fragrant, forested region rising out of the flat, dry prairie, and the Big Muddy — Saskatchewan's Badlands. The Big Muddy Badlands form a craggy landscape of jumbled rocks and caves which once sheltered cattle rustlers, whiskey runners and other outlaws — including, some say, Butch Cassidy.

Saskatchewan's distinctive plains and the formations to the far south were created by the action of the great glaciers which once covered large portions of the continent. Parts of Cypress Hills escaped the last ice age, and traces of the flora and fauna of that earlier epoch can be found here. The last glacier retreated between 20,000 and 8,000 years ago, leaving behind large inland lakes and meltwaters which cut enormous valleys in the land. Sedimentary deposits left by the lakes as they drained created the rich farmlands of the central sections of the province.

Although it is believed that migrants from Asia inhabited this area up to 40,000 years ago, no artifacts of these ancient peoples have been found. It is probable that the movements of the ice effectively obliterated all traces. Some evidence has been found of a nomadic buffalo-hunting people dated 6000 years ago, but much more is known of the Neo-Indian period, from 1-1600 A.D. The buffalo, or bison, meant everything to these early Plains Indians — food, clothing, housing, and even fuel for warmth and cooking. A culture was developed in keeping with the nomadic life of these Plains people, who followed the buffalo as they roamed the grasslands. With the coming of Europeans, around the late 17th century, the ancient way of life of both the plains and the northern tribes began to change.

As with the rest of Canada, the fur trade was instrumental in opening up Saskatchewan. In 1690 Henry Kelsey was instructed to make further explorations for the fur trade. He made the journey inland from his Hudson's Bay Company post, becoming the first European to view the Saskatchewan prairie.

As competition for the fur trade escalated, further inroads were made into the prairies, but it wasn't until 1812 that a small group of settlers arrived to start a colony at the head of the Red and Assiniboine Rivers, in what is now Manitoba. In 1870 the Red River settlement and environs entered Confederation as the Province of Manitoba; shortly after C. G. Archibald, the newly-appointed lieutenant-governor, began his administration of Manitoba and the Northwest Territories, of which the as-yet-unnamed Saskatchewan was a part.

In 1873 news of the 'Cypress Hills Massacre' reached the Canadian government in the east. An entire Assiniboine village, including women and children, was wiped out by a group of Canadians and Americans who had traced the theft of their horses to this village in the Cypress Hills. Public indignation at this outrage helped speed through a bill proposing a corps of 300 mounted police for the Northwest Territories. By 1875 a mounted police force was established at Fort Walsh, ending an era of lawlessness and illicit whiskey trade. The North West Mounted Police played an important role in the settlement of the west. They established good relations with the Indian tribes and were influential in negotiating a series of treaties, and in making the peaceful transition to an agricultural community.

By 1881 the census revealed that the area which is now Saskatchewan had a total population of 19,000. European and American settlers accounted for 1,000; 15,000 were Indians and 3,000 were of mixed blood. The hoped-for quick settlement of the west had not occurred, and in 1881 a bill was passed permitting the sale of land to colonization companies. At first these companies experienced a modest success, but this had dwindled by 1883. Nevertheless, a few struggling little communities had been established, and the coming of the railroad ensured support of these communities and the continuation of settlement.

Meanwhile, the coming of the railroad, the decline of the buffalo, and the influence of European immigration combined to force the Indian and Metis out of their traditional lifestyle. Threatened by this, the Metis invited their old leader, Louis Riel, back from the United States. When Riel set up a provisional government and took up arms to reinforce the Metis' claims with the government, troops were rushed from the east to smother the rebellion. The final battle was fought in 1885, at Batoche. Riel was later tried and executed, and other leaders of the rebellion were imprisoned. The rebellion was the last stand of the free-roaming Metis against the encroachments of the agricultural community. The old way of life had irrevocably changed. Today the North West Rebellion and the trial of Louis Riel are remembered in historic sites at Batoche, and in Regina, where the trial of Louis Riel is re-enacted on stage each summer.

The disappointingly slow settlement had been further hindered by the Northwest Rebellion. Accordingly, in 1896, the government embarked on a determined campaign to attract settlers from Europe and North America.

Flyers were sent out and advertisements issued, and the people came, attracted by the promise of free homesteads for agricultural use, and the fertility of the land. Many Eastern European settlers came: Belgian, Russian, German, Polish, Ukrainian and Rumanian. One of the most influential groups of settlers came from the United States. Of German, Belgian, Hutterite and Mennonite stock, these immigrants had usually been in America long enough to learn the language, familiarize themselves with farming and to establish definite aims. The land was indeed fertile, but the hardships of the climate and the isolation were a rigorous proving ground for these pioneers. It took physical hardiness, enormous courage and implacable strength of spirit to withstand these tests, a legacy which has been handed down to their descendants.

With this influx of people, the need for essential services became evident. Roads, schools, and cultural, medical and recreational facilities were needed as the area expanded in population and complexity. The difficulty lay in obtaining funds from the government in distant Ottawa. Provincial status would give the population control over much-needed funds. In 1897 the territorial government won control over financing but still did not possess control of the land or its resources. On September 1, 1905, the Province of Saskatchewan was created. The ceremony was held in Regina, and was attended by the NWMP and marked by great pomp and pageantry. But the problems did not end with the gaining of provincial status. The first half of the century proved to be a harsh testing ground for the province and its new-won independence.

After the First World War, Saskatchewan returned to a peacetime economy and a steady growth in the towns and cities which formed the nucleus of the agricultural belt. The establishment of Wheat Pools — an effort to control fluctuating wheat prices and give the farmer a measure of security, the development of new and better strains of wheat, agricultural education programs, and advances in farm machinery combined to create positive changes in the farm community. But by the end of the 1920s, the province was beginning to feel the effects of the world-wide depression.

Coincident with the depression, which created massive unemployment and drastically reduced the price of grain, came the severe drought which was to have such an enormous impact on the southern portion of the province. Saskatchewan's fine topsoil, with no moisture to hold it down, drifted away in huge, black clouds on the prairie wind, and with it went the hopes and dreams of many. Each year, faith in the rains which never came grew a little less. Abandoned farms and machinery became a familiar sight in southern Saskatchewan, symbols of the dreams left behind as farmers relocated.

Just when this period was ending, Canada declared war. Rationing was imposed throughout the country, and a farm labour shortage occurred as scores of young men went off to fight in Europe. In 1944, as the Second World War drew to a close, Saskatchewan elected the first socialist government in Canada.

Returning soldiers were greeted with a re-vitalized economy, a technology which had grown by leaps and bounds, and a new government. Having survived a rocky transition to an agricultural economy, a drought, and a war which depleted the labour force, Saskatchewan looked with a renewed vigour towards the future.

The post-war era was a time of rapid growth and expansion. The discovery of oil, the development of service and supply industries to support this find, and the later discovery of potash, helium, uranium, and the production of natural gas have given Saskatchewan a broader economic base, although agriculture is still its primary industry. Today the province is Canada's second largest producer of crude oil and uranium.

Potash and oil are the second and third largest industries in Saskatchewan. There are 9 potash mines across the province and oil rigs are much in evidence throughout the south. The forests of the north supply a thriving pulp and paper industry, and coal, first used by the settlers to heat their houses, and mined for commercial purposes since about 1910, is still a major industry.

Today neatly marked off farms crisscross the once immeasurable plains. The undulating waves of grass that were home to the bison have given way to rippling stands of wheat and other crops. Wheat is still the main crop of Saskatchewan but the wheatfields are interspersed with other crops such as flax, rye and canola.

This peaceful, ordered land now gives little indication of the backbreaking labour that went into turning the sod and taming the land to agricultural use. The fertile fields reveal little of the heartbreak of the 'dirty thirties'. But the strength of character and the courage of their forebears are embedded in the character of the people of this province. A strong independence is allied with the spirit of co-operativism that was once the key to survival in a harsh land. As an era of growth and prosperity settles in Saskatchewan, the rich cultural mixture of its people has become an asset, as various groups celebrate their ethnic origins in a land they have made very much their own.

The Western Red Lily, Saskatchewan's floral emblem.

Many of Saskatchewan's first settlers were immigrants from eastern Europe, and the prairies are dotted with churches of a variety of faiths. Above is St. Mary's Romanian Orthodox Church, near Kayville.

Grain elevators line a Kamsack street.

The sun sets through the dust of readying the ground for spring planting, near Fox Valley.

Saskatchewan is Canada's second largest producer of crude oil. Oil pumps
such as this one near Gull Lake dot the prairie landscape.

The St. Elizabeth Mission, near Hodgeville.

The Legislative Buildings at Regina were completed in 1912. This aerial photo shows the buildings designed in the form of a cross, and surmounted by a dome.

Opposite: A dramatic night view of Regina's City Hall. Begun in 1882 as a small settlement known as 'Pile-of-Bones', Regina is today the capital and largest city of the province.

Spectacular sunsets, such as this one on a northern lake, are a Saskatchewan trademark.

Windsurfers take advantage of summer's sun at Saskatchewan Landing Provincial Park, one of three parks located on the shores of Lake Diefenbaker.

One of Saskatoon's many bridges frames the turreted Bessborough Hotel, once part of the CN chain of hotels, and built in 1931.

Opposite: The spire of St. Andrew's Presbyterian Church gleams against the threatening sky of a summer thunderstorm.

Saskatchewan summers are marked by numerous festivals. Here the chuckwagon races at Duck Lake celebrate the pioneer history of the province.

Rising out of a flat, semi-arid region near Eastend, Cypress Hills extends westward for 100 kilometres, a verdant forested region of rolling hills and lakes. Above are the Ravenscrag Buttes, near the eastern end.

Lowering thunderclouds contrast dramatically with this grain elevator spotlighted by the sun.

Mud, manure and straw stucco on an old log building.

Opposite: The pioneer homestead of John Diefenbaker, Prime Minister of Canada from 1957 to 1963, is now a public museum.

These young cowboys carry on the tradition of the old west.

Opposite: Ice Fishing on Fishing Lakes near Fort Qu'Appelle. Well-utilised in all seasons, Fishing Lake has the longest stretch of white sand beach in Saskatchewan.

Waskesiu, in Prince Albert Provincial Park, has long been one of the favourite
vacation spots in the province, and boasts full recreational facilities.

Power boats line the sandy beach at Jackfish Lake, near The Battlefords Provincial Park.

The church and graves at Batoche. The Battle of Batoche ended the North West Rebellion in 1885, and the rectory here, along with the church, battleground and village of Batoche, have been declared a National Historic Site.

Opposite: An imposing grey stone church overlooks peaceful gardens in Moose Jaw.

Built in 1917 as a replica of the 1903 original, this structure was a residence for Peter Veregin, leader of the Doukhobors, as well as a prayer home. This stately mansion at Veregin is a museum, and the main floor continues to be used as a prayer home.

This reconstruction of Abe Farwell's original trading post at Fort Walsh was built in 1967 as part of Canada's centennial celebrations.

Teepee poles on a lonely hill mark the grave of Chief Poundmaker, who wanted peace between his people and the settlers.

Remains of barns of this unusual design are found occasionally throughout the prairies.

The Ipsco Steel Refinery, at Regina.

Opposite: Coal-mining at Bienfait. Strip mining once devastated the landscape in this coal-rich area, but reclamation projects were initiated in the 1970s. The sites are ploughed and reseeded, and many become pastures and wildlife preserves.

Grain elevators, first introduced in Saskatchewan at the turn of the 20th century, take advantage of gravity and grain's flow qualities. Here the grain is being dumped into the pit, where a conveyer will carry it to a storage area.

At harvest time, combines such as this one near Gravelbourg sometimes work night and day.

Gentle hills and the colours of autumn combine to create a landscape of subtle beauty near Hart.

Saskatchewan is home to a great variety of animal and bird species. Clockwise from upper left: pronghorn antelope, bison (these once numerous beasts are now protected in special compounds), whitetail deer, burrowing owl.

Fishing on Black Lake, near the border with the Northwest Territories. Water accounts for one-eighth of the surface area of Saskatchewan, most of it lying in the northern, sparsely populated half of the province.

Spectacular Nistowiak Falls, on the Churchill River, are some of the highest in the province.

A Yellow-headed Blackbird perches on cat-tails.

The shores of McKay Lake show the typical forest growth of Saskatchewan's northern sector.

Diefenbaker Lake was created in 1967 with the completion of the Gardiner Dam, Canada's largest earth-fill dam. The lake supplies irrigation and hydro-electric power, and the creation of three provincial parks along its shore has provided an excellent recreational source.

The Great Sand Hills, in southwestern Saskatchewan, is a 700 square mile (1,813 square kilometre) area of shifting sand, a fascinating region which is devoid of human habitation, but shelters many animal species.

The RCMP Musical Ride celebrates the important role of the RCMP (originally the North West Mounted Police) in the settlement of the west.

Opposite: Fort Battleford National Historic Park. The Commanding Officers Residence in the background is one of five original buildings still standing at Battleford.

These aerial photos show the fascinating designs created by cultivation of the land.

Fort Walsh was first established in 1875 to suppress the whiskey trade and to establish peaceful contact with the Indians of the area. Abandoned in 1883, the original buildings were reconstructed in 1944, when Fort Walsh was declared a National Historic Site.

This statue at Fort Walsh commemorates the good relations established with the Indians under the leadership of Superintendent James M. Walsh.

A spectacular sunset transforms a typical prairie scene of grain elevators and railway tracks.

The first snow of winter outlines the roof of the railway station at Rockglen.

Sunrise tints the snow-clad Cactus Hills a delicate pink.

Stubblefields form a backdrop to this snowbank sculpted by the wind, west of Regina.

Hoarfrost coats the trees along a peaceful country road south of Saskatoon.

Domed Ukrainian church near Sheho.

Opposite: Grain elevator looms out of the sunset mist at St. Walburg.

Photographic Credits